LAND TRANSPORTATION

Malcolm Dixon

Illustrated by
Jones Sewell and Associates

The Bookwright Press
New York • 1991

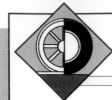

Technology Projects

Houses and Homes
Communications
Flight
Land Transportation
Machines
Structures
Textiles
Water Transportation

First published in the
United States in 1991 by
The Bookwright Press
387 Park Avenue South
New York, NY 10016

First published in 1991 by
Wayland (Publishers) Ltd
61 Western Road, Hove
East Sussex BN3 1JD, England

Library of Congress Cataloging-in-Publication Data
Dixon, Malcolm.
  Land transportation / Malcolm Dixon.
    p.   cm. — (Technology projects)
  Includes bibliographical references and index.
  Summary: Demonstrates the principles behind various forms of
transportation through projects for making wheels, cars, a motored
vehicle, a locomotive, and other vehicles.
  ISBN 0–531–18412–9
  1. Motor vehicles—Juvenile literature.   [1. Motor vehicles.
2. Transportation.   3. Science projects.]   I. Title.   II. Series.
TL147.D58   1990
629.04′9—dc20   90-22717
                                                           CIP
                                                           AC
Phototypeset by Nicola Taylor, Wayland
Printed in Italy by G. Canale & C.S.p.A.

Cover: *A four-wheel-drive vehicle
bounces across rough terrain in the
Paris–Dakar Rally.*

Contents

On the move

In our modern world people are often on the move. We travel by road and rail to get to school or work, to visit friends, do the shopping and go on vacation. All over the world goods are transported by freight trains and trucks. There are millions of cars, trucks, buses, bicycles and trains traveling over a vast network of roads and railroads.

The development of motorized forms of land transportation – such as cars, buses and trains – has made it much easier to travel from place to place, and this has changed many people's lives. One hundred and fifty years ago most people worked very close to where they lived, and they could buy only products that had been made or grown locally. Today people are able to live a long distance from their place of work and commute each day. The goods that we buy in our local stores have often

We rely on many different forms of land transportation in everyday life.

Computers are now very important in the design of vehicles. This engineer is using computer graphics to check the design of a new braking system.

been brought from a long way away. These changes have happened quite quickly, so quickly that they are sometimes called a revolution. This "transportation revolution" has not ended yet, because people are still finding faster and better ways of traveling on land.

Making road vehicles and trains that can move at high speeds, and yet be safe and comfortable to travel in, is a very complicated job. The designers and engineers who do this job have many different things to consider, such as the best materials to use, the correct type of engine to provide the power and the ideal shape for the vehicle. They need to consult books and discuss their ideas with other people, and they must plan everything in advance. There are always many problems to be overcome before the vehicle they have designed is ready to be put to practical use.

This book explains how many different types of vehicles work, and gives you the opportunity to make models of them, which will move on land. You will be able to build models from your own designs and to solve problems as they arise. There are chapters on how roads and railroad systems are built, the importance of safety in the design of transportation systems, and the ways in which methods of moving on land might change in the future.

The wheel

The wheel is one of the greatest inventions of all time. When early humans wished to move a heavy load they may have just dragged it. Later they discovered that rollers made the movement of a load easier. Rollers do not have to slide over the ground, so there is less friction. Logs of wood were placed under the load, and as the load was pushed forward, new rollers were placed in front of the load. This method was effective but slow.

It is believed that the wheel was first used about 5,000 years ago, in the Middle East, by the Sumerians. Their first wheels were probably made from solid disks of wood, but there is archaeological evidence that they also used wheels made of three pieces of wood, clamped together by cross-struts. At first, carts were made with two wheels on one axle, but later, carts with four wheels and a pair of axles were developed. Oxen were used to pull the carts. This type of wheeled transportation spread to Europe and to China.

About 4,000 years ago a new type of wheel was produced. It consisted of an outer rim connected by spokes to a hub at the center. This design, which is light but strong, was very suitable for horse-drawn chariots and wagons.

Today wheels are everywhere and they are used in many different ways. Think of as many uses as you can for wheels. Collect pictures from newspapers and magazines to show some of the many uses of wheels in land transportation.

Wheels like those on this cart have been in use for around 4,000 years.

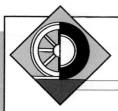

Making wheels

You need:
8 wooden Popsicle sticks (all the same size)
Cardboard
Pair of compasses
Scissors
White glue and a spreader
Hand-drill and ¼″ bit

Length of wood, ½″ square
Flat piece of wood about 6″ x 4″ x 1″
Hammer and small nails
Hacksaw
Dowel rod, ¼″ in diameter
Plastic tubing of ¼″ internal diameter

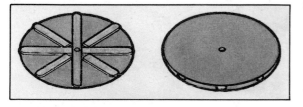

1. Measure the length of a Popsicle stick. Using the compasses draw two circles on a piece of cardboard; the diameter of the circles must be the same as the length of the stick. Carefully cut out the circles. Glue one stick to one cardboard circle, as shown. With the help of an adult drill a ¼″ hole through the center.

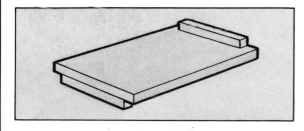

2. Next make yourself a bench-hook to help you cut the lengths of wood you will need. Nail or glue two strips of wood, each about 2½″ long by ⅜″ square, onto the flat piece of wood.

3. Use the bench-hook and a hacksaw (as on page 17) to cut three more sticks in half and stick the six pieces on the cardboard as shown. You will have to shorten them first so that they do not project beyond the circle. Now glue the second cardboard circle on top of the sticks. Let the wheel dry. Make a second wheel in the same way.

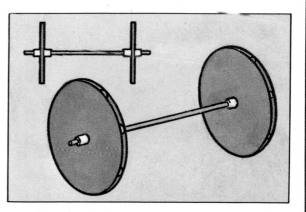

4. Cut four short pieces of the plastic tubing. Cut a piece of dowel rod about 6″ long to make an axle. Slide a piece of plastic tubing onto each end of the axle, then fit the wheels, and finally slide on the other pieces of plastic.

Bicycles and motorcycles

The bicycle is a human-powered form of transportation that is popular all over the world. The machines in use today have evolved from bicycles built over the last two centuries. In 1791 a wooden machine was built in France. The rider "walked" the machine along to make it move. The first pedal-pushed bicycle was built in 1839 in Scotland by a blacksmith, Kirkpatrick Macmillan. His design used foot pedals, which moved backward and forward, to drive connecting rods that turned the rear wheel. The "penny-farthing" bicycle was invented in 1871. It had a very large front wheel and a smaller rear wheel. The front wheel was driven by having the rider pedal cranks fixed to the center of the wheel.

Modern bicycles are driven by a

Modern racing bicycles are made of light, strong materials.

chain. A large sprocket, or chain wheel, is fitted onto the bicycle frame, and a smaller sprocket is fixed to the rear wheel. The two sprockets are connected by an endless chain. The rider turns pedal-cranks fitted to the larger sprocket. This moves the smaller sprocket and the rear wheel, and forces the machine to move.

The first motorcycle was built in France in 1869. A small steam engine was fitted to a bicycle with a pulley belt driving the rear wheel. Later designs used a gasoline engine connected by a chain drive to the rear wheel. Motorcycles are now a fast and economical form of transportation.

Looking at a chain drive

You need:
A bicycle

Look at the large sprocket on the bicycle. Notice how the pedals are fixed to it. Look carefully to see how the chain fits into the teeth of the large sprocket.

Ask a friend to lift the back wheel of the bicycle off the ground. Turn the pedals so that the large sprocket makes one complete turn. Notice how many times the back wheel turns. Now estimate how far the back wheel would travel for one turn of the large sprocket.

Count the number of teeth on the large sprocket. Count the number of teeth on the smaller sprocket. Can you see the link between these numbers and the number of times the back wheel revolves for one turn of the pedals?

Cars, buses and trucks

There are millions of cars on the world's roads. Their invention and production in huge numbers has revolutionized transportation systems. Many people now have the freedom to travel by car wherever they want, if a road or track is available.

Cars are built in a wide variety of shapes and sizes. Developing a new model from first designs through to mass production takes a great deal of work and is very expensive. Any new model of car includes many thousands of different parts, which must all work together to provide a safe form of transportation. The designers have to decide what size and type of engine is best to use for the vehicle they are building. They must consider whether the engine should drive the front or the rear wheels, and they must consider the brakes, the gearing, the steering, the suspension, the electrical system, the best materials to use and many other things. Prototypes will be built and tested. Finally, when the engineers are satisfied that the car is the best they can develop, then it will be made. Each day, thousands of new cars will be built on an assembly line using robots to fit the parts together.

Buses and trucks are just as important as cars in the world today. Modern buses can carry many passengers at great speed over long distances. Powerful trucks are used to move very heavy loads by road. Engineers are always working to make buses and trucks even better at their tasks.

Large trucks are used all over the world to transport goods by road.

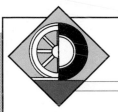

Make a model car

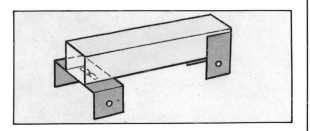

You need:
Long cardboard toothpaste box (or similar)
Rigid cardboard
Bench-hook (see page 7)
4 wheels (see page 7)
Dowel rod, ¼″ in diameter
Hacksaw
Scissors, ruler and pencil
Plastic tubing of ¼″ internal diameter
¼″ hole punch
Brass paper fastener
Glue (Elmer's or similar)

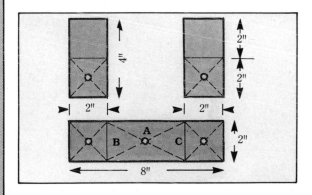

1. Cut out two pieces of rigid cardboard each measuring about 4″ x 2″. Mark the pieces as shown in the diagram and punch two holes where the diagonal lines cross.

2. Cut out another piece of rigid cardboard 8″ x 2″. Mark it as shown and punch holes where the diagonals cross. Make a small hole at point A and press the paper fastener through. Fold the cardboard along lines B and C.

3. Glue the two short pieces of cardboard to the outside of the box. Fix the large piece to the box with the paper fastener. It should be able to turn freely. These are the axle holders.

4. Using the bench-hook and a hacksaw, cut two pieces of dowel rod, one 4¾″ and one 6″ long. Push them through the holes in the axle holders. Make sure the longest axle goes through the widest axle holder. The axles should turn easily.

5. Make four wheels (use the method on page 7) and fix them to the axles using small pieces of plastic tubing. Now test your car. Does it move easily when you push it, and does the steering work? How can you make your car look more attractive? Try using paint, cardboard and other materials.

Providing power

To power a vehicle an engineer needs a suitable engine. The earliest engines used steam, produced by burning coal, to boil water in a closed tank. The steam was piped into the engine cylinders. This type of engine is called an external combustion engine because the source of heat is outside the engine. Most modern vehicles have internal combustion engines, in which the fuel is burned inside the cylinder. A mixture of fuel (usually gasoline) and air is sucked into a cylinder through an inlet valve as the piston inside the cylinder moves down. When the piston moves back up it compresses the fuel and air mixture, and a spark ignites the mixture. As the compressed mixture burns it expands and forces the piston down. The motion of the pistons moves a series of shafts and gears and eventually turns the

This is the engine of a powerful "hot rod." It runs on gasoline.

wheels of the vehicle.

Some vehicles use a type of internal combustion engine called a diesel engine. The fuel it runs on is not gasoline but diesel oil. The fuel mixture is ignited not by a spark but by the heat that is produced when air inside the cylinder is severely compressed by the piston.

The wankel engine is another type of internal combustion engine, which was developed quite recently. The wankel engine does not have cylinders or pistons. Instead, the fuel/air mixture is compressed by a rotor, a revolving part. That is why wankel engines are sometimes called rotary engines. Some vehicles do not use combustion engines at all but are powered by electric motors and batteries.

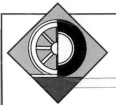

Using an electric motor

You need:
Screwdriver and small screws
Small electric motor
4.5-volt battery
Pieces of small electrical wire
Alligator clips
Flat piece of wood, about 4" x 6" x 8"
Thread spool with hole large enough to take the dowel snugly
Rubber bands
Plastic tubing of ¼" internal diameter
Hacksaw and scissors
Strong glue, e.g. Elmer's wood glue
¼" hole punch
Rigid cardboard
Dowel rod, ¼" in diameter
Paperclip to be used as a switch

1. Use glue or screws to fix the electric motor to the piece of wood. Fix a small piece of plastic tubing (or a blob of glue) to the end of the motor spindle.

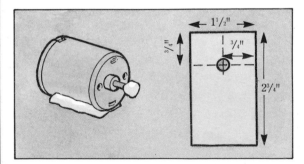

2. Cut two pieces of rigid cardboard 2¾" x 1½", and punch holes in them as shown. Glue the pieces of cardboard to the wooden baseboard.

3. Cut an axle from a piece of dowel rod long enough to fit through the holes in the cardboard pieces. First, push the spool onto the axle and glue it in the center. Pass a rubber band around the spool; the band should be very loose. Push the axle through the holes in the cardboard pieces and hold it in place with pieces of plastic tubing. Make sure the axle can spin freely.

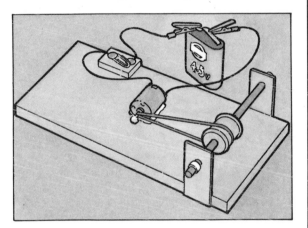

4. Attach the rubber band around the motor spindle. It should not be loose or too tight. If it doesn't fit properly you may have to try rubber bands of different lengths.

5. Strip the ends of the wires and attach a paperclip switch and a battery to the motor as shown. Switch on and see how the motor turns the rubber band, the spool and the axle. You can use this electric motor-driven system to drive the model on pages 14 and 15.

Make a powered vehicle

You need:
Bench-hook (see page 7)
Some lengths of wood, ⅜" square
Small electric motor
4.5-volt battery
Small electrical wire
Paperclips
Hacksaw
Thin cardboard
Rigid cardboard

White glue
Ruler, scissors and pencil
¼" hole punch
Dowel rod of ¼" diameter
Empty thread spool
4 wheels (see page 7)
Plastic tubing of ¼" internal diameter
Insulation tape
Large rubber band

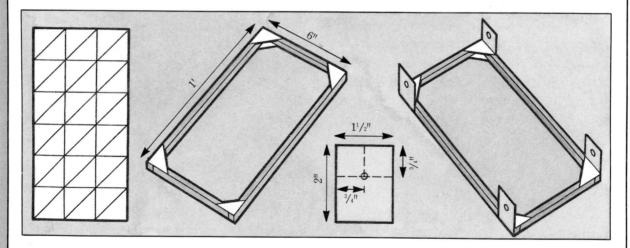

1. Use a pencil and ruler to draw horizontal, vertical and diagonal lines on a sheet of thin cardboard. Cut out these cardboard triangles as you need them.

2. Measure out two 6½" lengths of ⅜" square wood. Place your bench-hook on the table and use the hacksaw to cut through the wood on top of the bench-hook. Ask an adult to watch while you do this. Cut two 1' lengths of the ⅜" square wood using the same method.

3. Fix together the four pieces of wood you have cut to make a rectangular chassis. Make the corner joints by gluing the cardboard triangles and positioning them over the corners. Fix the triangles to both sides of each corner joint. Let the glue dry.

4. Cut four rectangles, 1½" x 2", from the rigid cardboard. Punch a hole in each piece, slightly off center. Glue one piece to each corner of the wooden rectangle. Let the glue dry.

5. Using the bench-hook and hacksaw, cut two 8½″ lengths of dowel rod. Slide a spool onto one of these dowel rod axles and place a rubber band around the spool. The band should hang loosely. Push the two axles through the holes in the cardboard pieces. Make four wheels (see page 7) and fix them on the axles with plastic tubing. Make sure the axles turn freely.

6. Cut two 6½″ length of ⅜″ square wood. Use glue and cardboard triangles to fix them inside the rectangular wooden chassis, about 1″ apart. Glue and tape a small electric motor to one of these lengths of wood. Put glue or a piece of plastic tubing on the end of the motor spindle and attach the loose end of the rubber band. The rubber band should not be loose or too tight.

7. Tape a 4.5-volt battery across the two wooden struts inside the chassis, next to the motor. Connect the battery to the motor using wire and paperclips.

8. Switch on the motor. Does it turn the rubber band, the spool, the axle and the wheels? Place your vehicle on the floor. Does it travel easily across the floor surface? Do you need to make any adjustments?

Design and make

9. Can you design and make a body shape for your vehicle? Use cardboard, clear plastic, paper and kitchen foil, etc., and fix your shape to the wooden chassis.

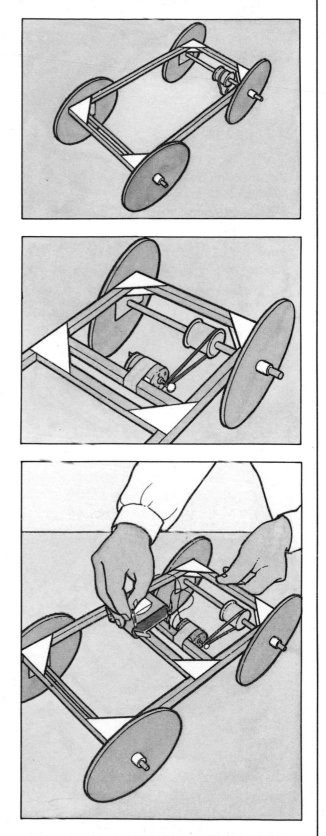

Gears

A gear is a wheel with small raised projections, called cogs or teeth, around its edge. The gears can be arranged so that their teeth interlock or "mesh" together. When two gears are meshed, turning one gear causes the other to rotate. Large gears have more teeth than small gears. When gears of different sizes are meshed, the smaller gear turns faster than the larger. A group of gears all working together is called a gear train.

Gears can be made from a variety of materials, including cast iron, steel and plastic, and they are used in many different ways. In a car, for example, the engine has a crankshaft, which rotates. The movement of the crankshaft is passed to the road wheels through a gear train called the transmission system. The gears transmit the motion of the engine to the wheels. The gears are of different sizes; the smaller gears provide greater power, and larger gears provide greater speed.

Most cars have a "gearbox" containing four or five forward gears and one reverse gear. The driver changes from one gear to another, using a gear lever attached to the gearbox. For more power, the driver selects a lower (smaller) gear; for more speed, the driver uses a higher (larger) gear.

Most cars have a clutch that disconnects the engine from the gearbox while the gears are changed. Today, many cars have automatic gearboxes, or transmissions, that change gear as the speed of the engine changes, so the driver does not have to use the clutch and gear lever.

The cogs on these two gears are interlocking, or "meshing."

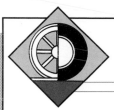

Making gears

You need:
2 circular cardboard cheese box lids (or similar)
2 nails
Hammer
Scissors
8 wooden Popsicle sticks
Flat piece of wood, about 1' long by 6" wide
White glue
Hacksaw
Bench-hook (see page 7)

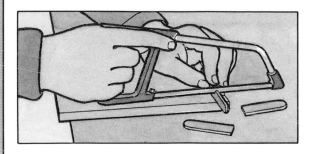

1. Cut the Popsicle sticks in half with the hacksaw on top of the bench-hook.

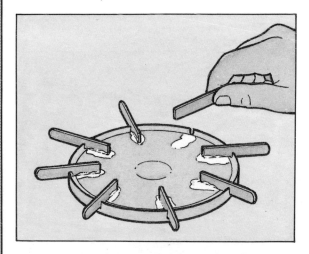

2. With scissors, cut eight slits at equal distances around the outer edge of each cardboard lid. Slide the half Popsicle sticks into the slits and glue them in place as shown. You now have two gears.

3. Make a hole in the center of each gear and lay the gears on top of the flat piece of wood as shown. Make sure the teeth mesh. Nail the gears to the wood and turn one of the gears. What happens to the other one?

Try making gears of different sizes. Mesh them together to make gear trains. Note that the gear's teeth *must have the same spacing*; the smaller gears will have fewer teeth.

Streamlining

Engineers spend a great deal of time and effort in ensuring that modern cars have streamlined shapes. A car with a streamlined shape can "slice" through the air. That means it will be able to travel faster and use less fuel. Car designers say that these cars have a low wind-resistance or low drag factor. If a car is designed to travel very fast it is vitally important that its tires stay in contact with the road, or the driver will lose control. So, in developing the shape of the car, the designers must make sure that as air passes over the car it presses downward.

Many ideas for ordinary road vehicles have been tested first as racing cars. Look at the picture of a racing car. As air passes over the front spoiler and rear wing it presses down and helps the car to grip the road. When you look at many modern cars you will see that they often have front spoilers, sloping front hoods and small rear wings. All of these design features allow the air to flow around the car and help with road-holding. Engineers often test the shapes of new car designs in a special wind tunnel to show that the air flows as smoothly as possible around them. Modern computer systems are now used in the design stages. They can calculate how air will flow around a car even before it has been built.

The spoiler and rear wing help to keep this racing car on the ground.

Investigating streamlining

You need:

Some wood, ⅜″ square
Bench-hook (see page 7)
Hacksaw
Scissors
Thin cardboard
Rigid cardboard, or posterboard

¼″ hole punch
White glue, such as Elmer's
Wooden Popsicle sticks
Dowel rod, ¼″ in diameter
Plastic tubing of ¼″ internal diameter
Hairdryer

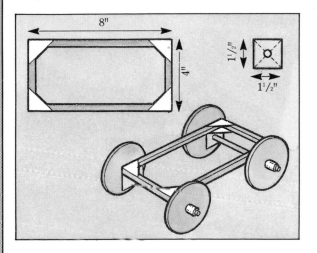

1. Using the method on page 14, make a chassis measuring 8″ x 4″ from the wood and triangles of thin cardboard.

2. Use some rigid cardboard to make four axle holders measuring ½″ square as shown and punch a hole in the center of each one. Glue the axle holders to the chassis as shown. Using the method on page 7, make four wheels of 3″ diameter from cardboard and Popsicle sticks. Cut two dowel rod axles 5½″ in length. Push the axles through the axle holders. Fix the wheels in position using small pieces of plastic tubing.

3. Design four different body shapes, which can fit over your vehicle chassis. Try different wheel sizes. Use thin cardboard and glue.

4. Plan an experiment to test the streamlining of the four car body shapes. Ask an adult to help you use a hairdryer to supply the "wind" for your experiment.

Supercars

Dragsters are built to be light, strong, streamlined and very fast.

Grand Prix racing takes place on specially designed circuits in various parts of the world. The cars that take part must be built according to international rules, which govern the engine size and other parts of the design. The cars are constructed using the most advanced techniques and materials. Because of the high speeds involved, any poor material or design idea is soon detected. Some of the ideas used in racing cars have also been used to build "supercars" to break the world land speed record. Malcolm Campbell, in 1935, traveled at 300 mph (480 kph) in his Bluebird car. More recently rocket-powered cars have traveled at 695 mph (1,120 kph).

Drag racing is a popular sport in the United States. A dragster is a special racing car designed to accelerate to a very high speed within a short distance. Some dragsters can move more than 1,300 feet (396 m) in less than six seconds. During this time they accelerate to over 200 mph (320 kph). They travel so fast that they often use a parachute to help them stop. The chassis of a dragster may be 25 feet (7.6 m) in length and be made of welded steel tubing. A strong but light design is required. Aluminum sheeting, which is also very light, covers the chassis, and careful streamlining ensures that the dragster stays on the ground at very high speed. Powerful engines, with superchargers and fuel injection systems, are used to give rapid accleration.

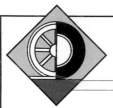

Make a dragster

You need:

Wood strip, ⅜″ square
Bench-hook (see page 7)
Hacksaw and scissors
Thin cardboard
Rigid cardboard
¼″ hole punch
Wooden Popsicle sticks
White glue, such as Elmer's
Dowel rod, ¼″ in diameter
Plastic tubing, ¼″ internal diameter
Hand-drill with ¼″ bit
Rubber bands

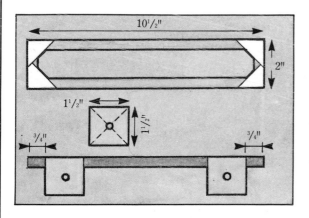

1. Using the bench-hook and hacksaw, cut two lengths of wood each measuring 10″, and another two each measuring 2″. Use the method shown on page 14 to make a chassis with the wood and some thin cardboard triangles.

2. Cut four axle holders 1½″ square from rigid cardboard. Punch a ¼″ hole in the center of each, and then glue them to the chassis.

3. Use cardboard and wooden Popsicle sticks to make two wheels of 2″ diameter and two wheels of 3½″ diameter. (Use the method on page 7.)

4. Cut two 3½″ lengths of dowel rod and push them through the holes in the axle holders. They should turn easily. Using pieces of plastic tubing, fit the smaller diameter wheels to one axle. This will be the front of your dragster. Fit the larger wheels to the back axle.

5. Loop some rubber bands together and attach them, by another loop, to the front of the chassis. Twist the other end of the rubber band around the back axle. Turn the axle around and around so that the rubber band is stretched quite tight. Place your dragster on a table top or on a level floor and then let it go. Does it move fast?

Road construction

A road has to be carefully planned before building starts. The planners first need the answers to many questions. How many vehicles will use the road? Will heavy trucks use it? How fast will the vehicles travel? What sort of weather will the road have to stand up to? Can the materials needed to build the road be obtained near to the site of the road? What materials will be used for the top surface of the road? The route that the road will take has to be mapped out and some buildings may have to be demolished.

The ground will be leveled by huge earth-moving vehicles (see page 34). Bridges and road tunnels may have to be built along the route of the road. To make the road foundations, layers of crushed stone and concrete will be used. To make it stronger, the concrete may be reinforced with steel mesh. In some parts of the world, large blocks of polystyrene have been used to make the foundations. Finally, a top surface of asphalt or concrete will be laid.

Many modern roads allow vehicles to travel at high speeds over long distances. In North America they are known as freeways or expressways. In Britain they are called motorways. They are carefully designed to be fairly straight, with no sharp bends or junctions.

This new road bridge is made of concrete reinforced with steel.

Make a concrete road

You need:
Soil
Long cardboard box
Small trowel
Small stones or gravel
Sheets of Styrofoam
Work gloves
Large, empty tin can

Sand
Cement powder
Bowl to mix concrete in
Bucket of water
Scissors
Chicken wire
Flat piece of wood
Sheet of polyethylene (plastic wrap)

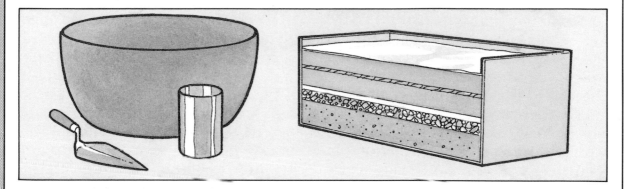

1. Put a layer of soil about 2½" deep in the cardboard box and flatten it down with the trowel. Place a layer of small stones on top of the soil and then cover the stones with a sheet of Styrofoam. The soil, stones and Styrofoam will form the foundations for your road.

2. Now mix some concrete. First put your gloves on. Use the tin can as a measure, and measure out one can of cement powder, three cans of small stones and two cans of sand. Mix them all together in an old bowl. Stir in some water – not too much, as the mixture should be quite stiff. Use the trowel or a piece of wood to mix all the materials thoroughly.

3. With the trowel, spread the concrete mixture over the foundations until it is fairly flat. Then tap the surface with the trowel to push out any air bubbles. Cut out a piece of chicken wire and lay it on top of the concrete.

4. Make some more concrete as before, and spread it on top of the chicken wire. Tap the concrete again to push out the air bubbles. Smooth out the surface and make it level using a flat piece of wood. Cover the concrete with a sheet of plastic wrap and leave it to harden.

5. Cut away one side of the box to show the layers of your road.

Building railroads

When traveling by rail, passengers can move around the carriages, eat in a restaurant and, if they wish, sleep. They are comfortable and safe. They can travel from city center to city center at high speed without the worry of traffic jams. Freight trains carry goods long distances across the world. Today, railroads are an important part of our lives.

Railroads were developed in Britain over 190 years ago, and they soon spread to other countries, especially the United States. Railroads are built over vast distances, through forests and across swamps and prairies. Tunnels are dug through mountains and under rivers, and bridges are constructed to carry railroads across waterways, roads, gorges and other railroad lines. Railroad engineers try to keep the railroad track as level as possible so that the train wheels do not slip on sloping tracks. Where the land begins to slope downward an embankment is built. This is a bank of earth with a flat top on which the railroad lines are laid. When hills have to be crossed the engineers dig through them to form cuts.

Modern trains run along steel rails that are fastened to cross ties made of heavy timber or concrete. These ties are laid on a foundation of broken stones, called ballast. Firm foundations are needed to support the huge weight of the trains on the rails. In hot weather the steel rails can expand. This could cause them

Railroad builders in the United States had to cross wild terrain.

A modern electric train crosses a bridge in a mountainous area of Japan.

to buckle and force trains off the rails, resulting in serious accidents. To prevent this, small gaps are left where two rails join. The two rails are held together by a pair of metal "fishplates." When you travel in a train you can often hear the clatter as the wheels pass over these gaps. Modern steel rails are welded together to form very long lengths. These rails are firmly fastened to heavy ties and fewer expansion gaps are needed. This makes train journeys much quieter.

The wheels of a train are made of steel and have a lip, or flange, on the inside edge. These flanges help trains to stay on the rails even when traveling around curves.

When you next travel on a train think of the problems the engineers may have had building the railroad. Watch for embankments and cuts. How many tunnels do you travel through? Do you travel under a river or through a mountain? How many bridges do you cross? Do you climb or descend any slopes? Look for passenger and freight trains. Listen to the sound of the wheels passing along the rails. Can you hear the regular clatter of the gaps in the rails or are you traveling on the modern welded rails? Find a safe position to look at some railroad tracks. Are the ties made of wood or concrete? **Never go near railroad lines**.

High-speed trains

The French TGV trains are some of the fastest in the world.

Railroads have to compete with road and air travel for passengers. There is, therefore, a need to make trains that can go faster than ever before. In Japan electric-powered "bullet" trains regularly run at 130 mph (210 kph) between Tokyo and Osaka. The French have developed trains that can travel at 170 mph (275 kph). Many engineers believe that this speed is close to the limit for trains riding on rails. New developments for high-speed rail vehicles may do without wheels and use air-cushion lift (see page 32) or a system of magnetic levitation.

Trains using the magnetic levitation (or maglev) method have already been built and are operating in Japan. Powerful superconducting magnets, cooled by liquid helium, are used to lift and propel the train along the track. When fully developed, these trains may be able to run at over 250 mph (400 kph). The ride will be smooth and almost silent because there will be no friction of wheels against the rails. Early maglev designs used a central guiding rail whereas newer plans suggest that the train will run between guiding walls.

Make a maglev train

You need:
Plasticine
2 strong bar magnets
Used matchsticks
Thin cardboard
Scissors

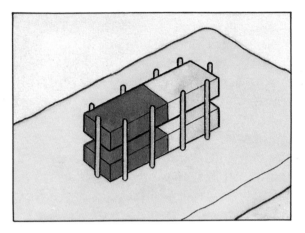

1. Roll out the Plasticine to make a long, flat slab about 3" x 6".

2. Place one bar magnet on the slab. Push some matchsticks into the Plasticine around the edges of the magnet.

3. Take the second magnet and try to make it "float" above the first magnet. Can you feel the force pushing them apart? Why do you need the "wall" of matchsticks? Try the experiment without the matchsticks in place.

Design and make
4. Using thin cardboard design and make a small train to fit on top of the floating magnet. Make the shape streamlined.

Cable railways

Cable railways are often used to transport passengers up steep slopes such as the sides of a mountain. The wheels of a conventional train would be unable to grip the track and would slide backward. Usually a double track is built up and down the mountain. The cable cars, which are like small railroad cars, are linked together by cables. When one car is at the top of one track the other is at the bottom of the second track. An engine is used to pull the cable and move the cars up and down the track. This type of cable car system is called a funicular railway.

In some mountainous areas, such as Switzerland, another type of cable railway, with aerial cable cars, is used. Strong steel pylons are built on deep concrete foundations, and steel cables are stretched between them. Large cable cars, sometimes carrying a hundred passengers, are suspended from these cables. Electric motors move the steel cables, transporting the cable cars up and down the mountain. Safety is very important because some pylons are spaced 1 mile (1.6 km) apart and the cables may be 1,000 feet (300 m) above ground level. Chair lifts, which carry single or twin seats, are another type of cable transportation. They are often used by skiers.

Aerial cable cars can carry many people up and down mountains.

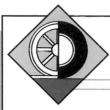

An aerial cable car system

You need:
Some lengths of wood, ¼″ square
Bench-hook (see page 7)
Hacksaw and scissors
White glue, such as Elmer's
Wooden Popsicle sticks
Thin cardboard
Pair of compasses
Rigid, thick cardboard
¼″ hole punch
Hand-drill and ¼″ bit
Dowel rod, ¼″ in diameter
Plastic tubing
String
Thin wire
Baseboard of wood or thick cardboard

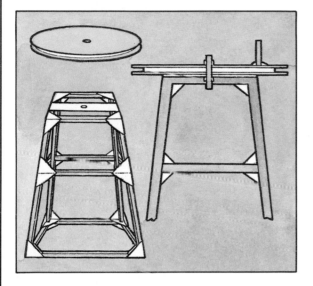

1. Build two pylons as shown out of wood and cardboard triangles. Glue Popsicle sticks to the framework to provide extra strength. Glue a piece of rigid cardboard, with a ¼″ hole punched in the center, across the top of each pylon.

2. Make two pulley wheels out of circular pieces of cardboard. For each wheel, glue thin cardboard circles to both sides of a slightly smaller circle of thick cardboard. Drill a hole through the center of each wheel.

3. Fix one pulley wheel to the top of each pylon, using dowel rod and plastic tubing. Glue a small piece of dowel rod to the top of one pulley wheel to act as a turning handle.

4. Connect the two pylons together with strong string running around the pulley wheels. You may need to glue the ends of the string together.

5. Design and make some cable cars. Use paper or thin cardboard so that they are light. Hang the cable cars from the string using thin wire.

6. Turn the dowel rod handle and make the cable cars move. Glue the pylons to a baseboard.

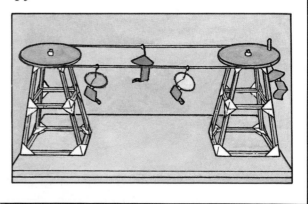

Amphibious vehicles

An amphibious vehicle emerging from the sea onto the land.

Amphibious vehicles, sometimes called amphibians, can move both in water and on land under their own power. Many of these vehicles have been developed for military use. They are able to float in water and move using small propellers or water jets. On land, wheels or tracks are used for movement.

Air-cushion vehicles (ACVs), or hovercraft, are also able to move on land and on water. A hovercraft hovers just above the road or water surface supported by a cushion of air. A powerful hovercraft can travel much faster on water than a large boat, and far faster than most other amphibious vehicles. It has the great advantage of being able to move from sea to land easily. Once on land, hovercraft can operate well over very smooth surfaces. They are not yet very successful over snow or rough ground. The air cushion is produced by propellers driven by powerful motors. It is kept under the hovercraft by a flexible "skirt" that hangs around the edge of the vehicle. The hovercraft is pushed along by other propellers and steered by rudders that deflect the airstream.

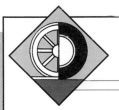

Make a hovercraft

You need:

Light, shallow plastic or foam container
Marker pen
Small electric motor
Sticky tape, such as Scotch tape
Scissors
Wire and wire stripper
Paperclips
Small plastic propeller
White glue, such as Elmer's
4.5-volt battery

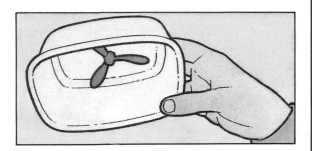

3. Glue the propeller to the motor spindle. The propeller should turn without touching the sides of the container.

4. Place your hovercraft on the floor and attach the paperclips to the battery. Does your hovercraft lift off the floor?

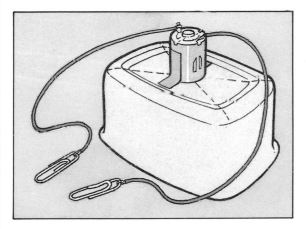

1. Find the exact center on the bottom of the container by making diagonals as shown. Make a small hole where they cross.

2. Push the spindle of the electric motor through this hole and tape the motor in position. Cut two lengths of wire and remove the insulation from the ends using the wire stripper. Fasten one wire to each of the two motor connections. Fix a paperclip to the free end of each wire.

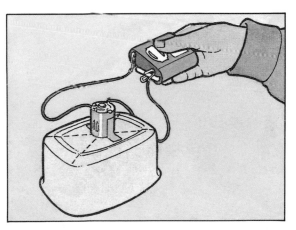

Design and make

5. Design and make a skirt to go around the edge of your hovercraft. Decide what materials would be best to use. How can you fix the skirt to the hovercraft? The skirt should make your hovercraft lift farther off the floor.

Earth-moving vehicles

When engineers are building roads and railroads, they have to move millions of tons of earth from the site. Special vehicles have been built to help them. Scraper and grader machines are often used. The scraper is a vehicle with a knife-like cutting blade that can slice off layers of soil and rock. The depth of the layer of earth to be scraped off can be varied by adjusting the cutting blade. The earth that is removed is forced into a large container inside the vehicle and then transported to a dumping site. Large diesel engines can provide these vehicles with tremendous power. Huge wheels and tires help them to move around on rough terrain. When most of the earth has been removed from the site, grading vehicles set to work. A grader also has a cutting blade. It produces a more precise, flatter finish to the surface.

Bulldozers are used all over the world to move earth and make land flat. Crawler tracks allow bulldozers to move easily over very rough ground. Like scrapers, bulldozers are powered by diesel engines. There is a large blade at the front of the vehicle to push loads.

This bulldozer is pushing a large load of soil with its blade.

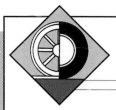

Make a bulldozer

You need:
Cardboard boxes
Thin cardboard
White glue, such as Elmer's
Bench-hook (see page 7)
Hacksaw
Dowel rod, ¼″ in diameter

Foam pipe insulation
4 empty thread spools of equal size
Plastic tubing of ¼″ internal diameter
Corrugated cardboard
Thick cardboard
4 paper fasteners

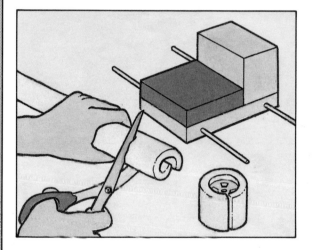

1. Glue together some cardboard boxes and thin cardboard to make a bulldozer shape.

2. Make four holes near the base of the bulldozer. Using the bench-hook and hacksaw, cut two dowel rods to act as axles. Push them through the holes and make sure that they turn easily.

3. Cut some pipe insulation into four sections and fit each one around a spool. Push the spools onto the axles and fix them in place with pieces of plastic tubing.

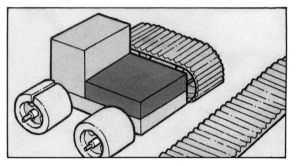

4. Cut two lengths of corrugated cardboard to make crawler tracks. Fit one track around each pair of wheels and glue the ends together.

5. Use thick cardboard to make the front blade of the bulldozer. Fix it to the bulldozer body with paper fasteners and thick cardboard. Push your bulldozer along. Does it move easily?

Brakes

The brake disks on this racing car are so hot they are glowing red.

You have discovered some of the ways in which vehicles can be made to move. But how do they stop? Many vehicles are fitted with brakes called "drum brakes." A foot pedal is connected to the brakes by small tubes containing compressed air or hydraulic fluid – liquid that is under pressure. When the pedal is pressed down, it pushes against the fluid or opens an air valve. This forces curved brake shoes against the inside of a rotating drum. When the brake shoes and the drum rub together, the friction slows down the rotation of the drum.

Disk brakes are now used on many modern cars. In these the air or fluid forces two brake pads onto the sides of a revolving disk, causing the disk to slow down. The materials used for brake shoes, drums and disks have to be tough and provide a great deal of friction.

Like cars, trucks and buses, railroad trains also use drum and disk brakes. They are usually operated by compressed air. But in this case, the brakes are applied when the air pressure is released. The air is passed down the entire length of the train through a pipe. When the air pressure is reduced, all of the brakes are applied at the same time. Have you seen the communication cord or alarm handle in a train? In an emergency, if the cord is pulled, compressed air is released from the pipe and the brakes are applied automatically.

A hydraulic brake system

You need:

2 flat pieces of wood
Hammer and nails
Empty shallow tin can
2 plastic syringes
Plastic tubing to fit syringes
Water
Sticky tape, such as Scotch tape

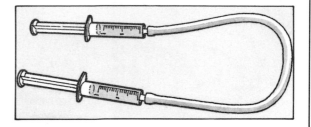

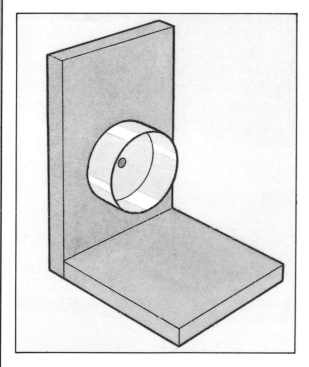

3. Join the syringes together with plastic tubing. Fill the tube and syringes with water – this is best done underwater in a sink, to prevent air bubbles from getting in. Press the plunger of one syringe. What happens to the other syringe?

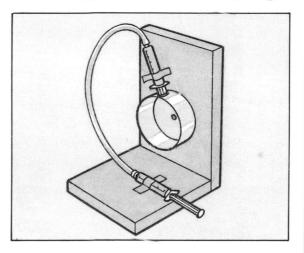

1. Fix the pieces of wood together to form an L-shape, using the hammer and nails.

2. Find the center of the base of the tin can and hammer a nail through it. Fix it loosely to the wooden upright as shown. Spin the tin can and make sure it revolves easily around the nail.

4. Fix one syringe to the wooden upright using Scotch tape. Then tape the other syringe to the baseboard. Spin the tin can and then press the syringe on the baseboard (imagine it is the brake pedal of a car). The plunger of the second syringe (the car brake) should be pushed against the tin can (the car wheel), forcing it to slow down.

Safety

While land transportation has developed, road vehicles and trains have been made to travel faster and faster. What is more, there are now more vehicles on the roads than ever before. Because of these factors, accidents happen every day. Engineers try to think of ways to reduce the number of accidents. Dual-circuit brakes and anti-lock braking systems, for example, have made some cars safer to drive.

Cars are designed to try to protect the driver and passengers if an accident occurs. Special safety glass is used in the windows. Some cars have rigid cages and body sections that crumple on impact, leaving the section in which people sit relatively undamaged. Seat belts also protect people in accidents, and collapsible steering wheels, padded head-rests and padded interiors all help to reduce injuries.

Markers called cat's-eyes in the road reflect light from car headlights to tell drivers which side of the road they are on. Crash barriers are used on divided highways and other fast roads to prevent vehicles from crashing into oncoming traffic. They are usually strong enough to keep vehicles from breaking through them. Traffic lights, sometimes controlled by computers, can reduce the number of accidents at road junctions.

Signaling systems are also used on railroads. They tell train drivers when to stop and when it is safe to go. Many railroad accidents have been caused by human mistakes. Automatic safety devices and computers are increasingly being used to reduce the chances of human error and prevent accidents.

A simulated accident. The dummies without seat belts are thrown forward.

An automatic signal system

You need:
Thin cardboard
Scissors
Kitchen foil
Glue
Wire
Wire stripper
4.5-volt battery
Bulb holder and 3.5-volt bulb

1. Cut a piece of cardboard measuring 8" x 3". Cut two pieces of kitchen foil 8" x 1". Glue the foil strips to the cardboard as shown.

2. Remove the insulation from the ends of two lengths of wire using the wire stripper. Push the wire-ends between the foil and the cardboard as shown. Make sure they are firmly fixed and that the wires are touching the foil. Carefully fold the cardboard along the dotted line. You have made an automatic switch.

3. Connect the other ends of the wires to the battery and bulb holder, and join the battery and bulb holder together with another piece of wire. Place your automatic switch on the floor or on the road you made (page 23). If you drive one of your vehicles over the switch the light should go on. It should go out again when the vehicle has passed. Try using a buzzer instead of the bulb. Can you figure out how this automatic signal system works?

Space exploration

People have already begun the exciting challenge of exploring space. Rockets and spacecraft have been developed and men have landed on the moon. In 1970 the USSR built and placed on the moon the first lunar vehicle, called Lunokhod 1. This robot vehicle was controlled by radio signals from earth. A large panel of solar cells made electricity from sunlight. The electricity was used to drive Lunokhod's eight wheels and control the television cameras and other scientific instruments that were carried on the vehicle.

The United States has also landed a vehicle on the moon. The Apollo 15 astronauts, Scott and Irwin, used a Lunar Roving Vehicle to explore the moon's surface. It was electric powered and had a maximum speed of 10 mph (16 kph). The wheels were made of wire mesh. Both astronauts were able to sit on the vehicle and could travel about 40 miles (65 km) if they wished. A television camera and antenna sent pictures back to earth. When the astronauts returned they left the vehicle on the moon.

This is the Lunar Roving Vehicle that was taken to the moon as part of the Apollo 15 mission.

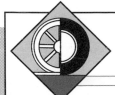

Make a planet-roving vehicle

The problem:

Design and build a model planet-roving vehicle. It must be able to carry two passengers and move over a planet's surface. Remember, there is no oxygen to run a gasoline engine and no air for tires.

Materials to use:

Empty washing-up liquid bottles
Pieces of wood, ½″ square
Plastic tubing of ¼″ internal diameter
Bench-hook (see page 7)
Hacksaw
White glue, such as Elmer's
Dowel rod, ¼″ in diameter
Rubber bands
Electric motor
4.5-volt battery
Paperclips and wire
Wooden Popsicle sticks
Thin cardboard and thick cardboard

The method:

1. Collect ideas – look through this book and at other books in libraries to find some ideas. Think how you might power your vehicle: with an electric motor or a stretched rubber band, perhaps. Will you use small or large wheels? What will you use to make the wheels? How big will you make the chassis?

2. Make drawings – as ideas come to mind, make sketches.

3. Select your best idea – think carefully about all of your ideas and decide which one you think will work best. Make an accurate drawing of the one you choose.

4. Construct your model – build the vehicle you have designed. First test it on a smooth surface and then try it on a rough surface. Have you solved the problem? How could you modify your model to make it work even better?

The future

Manufacturers are continually developing road vehicles that give better performance while using less fuel. In many advanced car engines the fuel is injected into the cylinder by special valves called fuel injectors. This gives more power than if the fuel is simply sucked in by the movement of the pistons. Special alloys, which are lightweight but strong, are used. Some cars are fitted with turbochargers, which use the normally wasted exhaust gases to boost the power of the engine. To reduce air pollution, a device called a catalytic converter can be fitted to the exhaust system of a car. These trends to improve performance, to reduce fuel costs and air pollution, to use new materials and to fit increasingly advanced computer systems, will almost certainly continue. Some people predict that in the future road vehicles will not need drivers because computers will be able to drive safely and find the correct route from place to place.

Gasoline engines may be phased out altogether and be replaced by ones that use a more "environmentally-friendly" fuel or by electric engines. Cars are now being developed that use electric engines for short-distance driving and a normal combustion engine for expressway travel. Public transportation may be improved with better and faster railroad and bus systems. The bicycle will continue to grow in popularity as a cheap and healthy form of transportation. As in the past, changes in land transportation methods will probably transform our lives.

Will cars of the future look like this?

Build a wind-powered vehicle

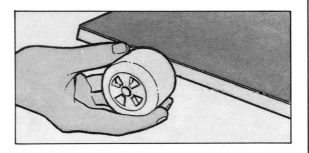

You need:

Wood, ⅜″ to ½″ thick for chassis
Bench-hook (see page 7)
Hacksaw
White glue, such as Elmer's
Scissors
Thin cardboard
Rigid cardboard
¼″ hole punch
6 empty thread spools
Dowel rod, ¼″ in diameter
Foam pipe insulation
Plastic tubing of ¼″ internal
diameter
Sheet of polyethylene (plastic film)

1. Build a chassis 10″ x 12″ using wood and thin cardboard triangles (see page 14). Glue a sheet of rigid cardboard to the top of the chassis. Glue two spools to the cardboard as shown.

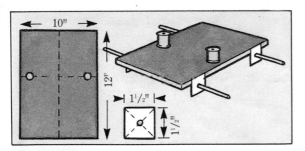

2. Cut four axle holders measuring 1½″ square out of rigid cardboard and punch a hole in the center of each. Glue the axle holders to the chassis. Cut two 12″ lengths of dowel rod and push them through the axle holders. They should turn easily.

3. Make four wheels using spools and pipe insulation (see page 35). Fit the wheels onto the axles and hold them in place with plastic tubing.

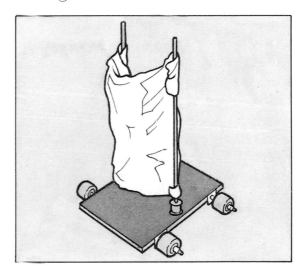

4. Cut two 12″ lengths of dowel rod to make masts. Push them into the spools on top of the model. Glue them firmly in place. Cut a square of polyethylene and stick it to the masts to make a sail. Test your model outside on a smooth area of concrete. How far does it travel? Do you need to make any modifications?

Glossary

Alloy A mixture of metals.

Anti-lock brakes A braking system designed to prevent skidding when the brakes are applied suddenly.

Assembly line A system in which workers or robots are each responsible for one job in the making of, for example, a car.

Axle The shaft to which the wheels of a vehicle are attached.

Brake A device used to slow down or stop a vehicle.

Catalytic converter A device fitted to a vehicle's exhaust system to reduce the amount of pollutants in the exhaust gases.

Chassis The framework on which a vehicle is built.

Clutch A device to disconnect a vehicle's engine from the gearbox.

Connecting rod A rod that transmits motion and force between a rotating part (which spins) and a reciprocating part (which moves back and forth).

Cylinder The tube inside which a piston moves in an engine.

Dual-circuit brakes (dual braking system) A braking system with two circuits; if one fails the other continues to operate.

Engine A device that converts one sort of energy into another.

Exhaust system The means by which exhaust gases are removed from an engine.

Friction A force that tends to prevent sliding between surfaces in contact.

Fuel A substance that produces energy in the form of heat.

Fuel injection system A way of pushing fuel into the cylinders of an engine.

Internal combustion engine An engine in which the fuel is burned in a cylinder to drive a piston.

Maglev Magnetic levitation.

Mass production Making identical objects in very large numbers.

Piston A part that moves up and down in the cylinder of an engine.

Prototype The first vehicle built to a new design.

Spoiler A device designed to use the pressure of moving air to hold a car firmly on the ground.

Supercharger A device, driven by the engine itself, that forces air into the engine and boosts performance.

Superconducting magnet A magnet made with superconductors so that a strong magnetic field can be maintained without continually using electric power

Superconductor Something through which an electric current can pass without any of the energy being lost.

Vehicle Any machine that can transport people or goods.

 **Further information**

Books to read

Algeo, Philippa, *On Wheels!* (Gareth Stevens, Inc., 1986)
Brandt, Keith, *Transportation* (Harcourt, Brace, Jovanovich, 1987)
Cain, Wilma, *Story of Transportation* (Gateway Press, 1988)
Lambert, Mark, *Car Technology* (Bookwright, 1990)
Pollard, Michael, *Train Technology* (Bookwright, 1990)
Steele, Philip, *Land Transport Around the World* (Dillon, 1986)
Unstead, R.J., *Travel by Road Through the Ages* (Dufour, 1967)

Organizations to contact

American Truck Historical Society
201 Office Park Drive
Birmingham, AL 35223
(205) 879–2131

American Trucking Association
2200 Mill Road
Alexandria, VA 22314
(703) 838–1700

Association of American Railroads
50 F Street, NW
Washington, D.C. 20001
(202) 639–2100

Modern Transport Technical and
Historical Society
P.O. Box 1458
Monrovia, CA 91016
(213) 335–5063

Transport Museum Association
3015 Barrett Station Rd.
St. Louis, MO 63122
(314) 965–6885

 **Places to visit**

Branford Trolley Museum
17 River St.
East Haven, CT 06
(203) 467–6927

Henry Ford Museum and
Greenfield Village
20900 Oakwood Blvd.
Dearborn, MI 48121
(313) 271–1620

Museum of Science and Industry
57th St. and S. Lake Shore Drive
Chicago, IL 60637
(312) 684–1414

Ohio Railway Museum
936 Proprietors Rd.
Worthington, OH 43085
(614) 885–7345

Smithsonian Institution
Museum of History and Technology
Constitution Ave. at 14th St. NW
Washington, D.C. 20560

Transit Museum
Boerum Pl. and Schermerhorn St.
Brooklyn, NY 11201

Index

Picture acknowledgments

The photographs in this book were supplied by: Allsport *front cover*, 8, 18, 20; Eye Ubiquitous 12, 25, 26, 32; Mansell Collection 24; Quadrant 42; Topham 5, 6, 16, 28 (Associated Press); Transport and Road Research Laboratory 38; ZEFA 4, 10, 22, 30, 34, 40.
All illustrations are by Jones Sewell and Associates.